MW00711196

EVERYTHING
IRISH

Also by Judy Wells

I Have Berkeley

Albuquerque Winter

Jane, Jane

Been in Berkeley Too Long
  with Carla Kandinsky
  Ralph Dranow
  Donna Duguay

The Part-Time Teacher

The Calling

EVERYTHING IRISH

POEMS BY
JUDY WELLS

Scarlet Tanager
BOOKS

Copyright ©1999 by Judy Wells
All rights reserved
Printed in the United States of America

Library of Congress Catalog Card Number:
98-75205

ISBN 0-9670224-0-1

Cover art: An adaptation of the initial "D" from
Collectio Canonum, Cologne Cathedral Library,
Germany © Classic Designs Ltd, 1992
Reproduced with permission by L.J. Young, Publisher
The Mills, Blarney, Co. Cork, Ireland

Cover Design: Judy Wells, Dale Jensen, Scott Perry

Book Design: Scott Perry of Archetype Typography

Back cover photo: Olivia Eielson

Typography: Archetype Typography, Berkeley, CA

Published by Scarlet Tanager Books
P.O. Box 20906
Oakland, CA 94620

Dedication

To the whole Irish contingent:

Edward A. Rodgers, Gortin, Co. Tyrone
Letitia Kinney Rodgers, Philadelphia
Anna Rodgers Smith, San Francisco
Irene Smith Wells, Agnes Smith, Bob Smith
Melinda Kavanagh, Nancy Brewer, Mel Wells, Jr.
and
All their children
who may want to claim
their Irish roots

Bridget Connelly and Sarah Fike

And my Viking
Dale Jensen

Acknowledgments

I would like to thank the following publications in which my poems appeared: *Beatlick's Nashville Poetry Newsletter*: "Confessions of a Counselor"; *Chameleon*: "Hope"; *Coffeehouse Poetry Anthology*: "Confessions of a Counselor," "Hope"; *The Crazy Child Scribbler*: "We Were the Cause of Our Second Grade Teacher's Nervous Breakdown"; *Howling Dog*: "The Seminar"; *Sophia*: "Everything Irish About Me in a Nutshell," "How I Learned Poetry, Theology, and Grammar All on the Same Day in 6th Grade"; *Southwest Women's Poetry Exchange*: "Light as the Holy Ghost"; *To Honor A Teacher*: "My Spiritual Life"; *The Walrus*: "What We Forgot," "English Test."

Thanks also to Nancy Brewer for research, Bridget Connelly for editing, Olivia Eielson for photography, and Lucy Day and Dale Jensen for encouragement.

Contents

HUNGER

PATRICK KAVANAGH MARRIES

Foreword

When I was in sixth grade, Sister Placidus was always saying, "Napoleon was the only one who could do two things at once, so don't you try, young lady." I never knew where she got that information, but it was confirmed many years later, when I had fled my Catholic Girlhood. Napoleon indeed could do two things at once; and I am sure Sister Placidus didn't know that one thing was affairs of Sex and the other thing was affairs of State.

It was then, long after six grade, I discovered that all sorts of truths half-understood by the nuns and all sorts of half-truths fully understood by the nuns were the staple of my spiritual diet. Theology class didn't matter; what mattered were monstrous sweet horrors handed out by the Old Country nuns. These are what I remember; these are what I cherish.

Judy Wells' collection, *Everything Irish,* says it all for me. She captures the times all of "Our Girls" were haunted by a wayward Holy Ghost, a perfect Holy Mary, a thundering Holy Father. She inspires me to remember the times Saint Anthony found everything for me (and still does), and PleaseGod got me out of a fix (and still does). I know exactly what she means when she says,

> and your lips get purser and purser
> and kapowie and kapowie inside…

because she means exactly, precisely, excruciatingly, that a Catholic Girlhood will never leave you even if you try to say goodbye.

Mary Norbert Körte

EVERYTHING IRISH IN A NUTShELL

EVERYTHING IRISH
ABOUT ME IN A NUTSHELL

My mother's church in San Francisco was called St. Brigid's, my church was called St. Catherine's, I was told I had the map of Ireland on my face, said "Mither, I want me mush" when I was a kid, my best friend in kindergarten was called Kathleen Ahern, I went to parochial school, wore a navy blue uniform and beanie, had priests called Monsignor Burke, Father Cushnahan, and Father Coffey in our parish, my smart girl rival in Catholic school was Marleen Dunne, Paul and Philip Murphy, the twins, were the milk boys at school, Darragh Flynn could run faster than me, I collected holy cards, hoarded silver dollars in my sock, was sexually repressed, committed minor sins but still thought I was going straight to hell, took the "pledge" when young, I think, I forget, I had an alcoholic uncle who was the family secret, I had very pale skin, blue eyes and dark hair, my childhood enemy was Marylou Mahoney down the street, her mother thought I was the ringleader against her daughter, I wore green on March 17th, said I was "English, Irish, and Scottish" when asked what I was, I went to Mass every Sunday, knelt down before the radio for rosary recitation, I sunburnt to a crisp, had a spinster schoolteacher aunt called Agnes, I never thought of going to Ireland, but went to France three times, my mother was a dyed-in-the-wool Democrat, feisty politico, go-straight-to-the-top type woman, her son was favored over three daughters, I love potatoes and sweets, and often feel I'm starving—that's everything Irish about me in a nutshell—except I'm always running late, love to chat, and I am a poet.

PAGAN BABIES

For Mary Norbert Körte, poet and ex-nun,
who told us there were no pagan babies.

Good evening!
I'm from the Police Athletic Association.
How are you this evening?
Are you interested in keeping
inner city kids off the street,
supporting wayward boys
      wayward girls
          pagan babies?

Pagan babies?
O my god!
Flashback! Flashback!
1955
St. Catherine's School
     J. M. J.
       +
Boys and girls, remember to hand in your
pagan baby envelopes today.
Boys and girls, we have enough money
to buy a pagan baby!
We need a name!
"Sister, Sister!"
Yes, James?
"James Patrick, Sister."
Very nice, James.
Any others, children?
Yes, Patrick?
"Patrick Thomas, Sister."
Very nice, Patrick.
Any others?
Maria?

4

"Maria Theresa, Sister."
Heads down on your desks, boys and girls.
All those for James Patrick? ✕✕✕✕ ✕✕✕✕ /
Patrick Thomas? ✕✕✕✕ ✕✕✕✕ ✕✕✕✕ ✕✕✕✕ ✕✕✕✕ ✕✕✕✕
Maria Theresa? //
Patrick Thomas is our new little pagan baby, boys and
    girls!
Another little baby boy is saved!

Who is he? Where is he?
Where are they?
All our little Irish-named pagan babies.
I thought they were from China.
We were saving souls from China
but who knows.
Maybe the mission
was just down the street
in the public junior high.

Recently I heard on KPFA
infanticide is common in China.
Baby girls
(pagan baby girls)
are unwanted in a culture
where one child is the rule.
Kris Welch heard about the baby girls
in the "dying rooms"
and wanted to adopt one
as did many Westerners.
Would they be called
Kathleen and Padraigin
and Megan
these new pagan babies?

Hand in your brown
envelopes, boys and girls.

It's time to stand up
and put your money
where your mouth is.
Good evening, ladies and gentlemen.
This is the Society
for the Propagation of the Faith.
Buy a pagan baby.
Think of all the starving people in the world.
Buy a pagan baby!
Buy a pagan baby!
Buy a pagan baby now!

WE WERE THE CAUSE OF OUR SECOND GRADE TEACHER'S NERVOUS BREAKDOWN

We were only eight years old
but we already knew
if we weren't good
we would die
      like Davey Murphy's sister
            a stomach bloated with cancer,
that Jessie May had seen the Angel of Death
          when her Grandma died,
     and that we were the cause
of our second grade teacher's nervous breakdown.

True, we were only seven years old
and had barely attained
the age of reason
      when we were accused.
True, there were fifty of us monsters
         in the classroom
and maybe we weren't reasoning all that well
so that was the year the angel
Sister Virginia Elizabeth
came to substitute
      and rescue us from sin.

She smelled like lemon soap,
had been a nurse nun
      and wore a snow white habit
         in her former life.
And that was the year I was lucky.
I won a little doll Sister Virginia Elizabeth
      sewed a snow white habit for
out of real nun's cloth
      with a cross and pockets.

And I won a big picture
	of Jesus with pretty long hair
		and a sacred heart.
It was much bigger
than the book mark-holy cards
		we usually got
and I know the other kids
		must have thought things were rigged
		but they weren't, were they, Sister?
I was just lucky that year.

Then I lost Jesus,
	the big picture.
He was in my desk one minute,
	gone the next.
And I knew someone took Him
	and Sister got Him back for me.
I can't remember whether
	it was Lolita or Lorraine
	but they were new
	and they were twins.

Lolita was the smart one.
	She was wiry and had straight
		short hair
and Lorraine was the dumb one.
She was big and placid
but I think it was Lolita
	who finally fessed up
		she took Jesus.

I wonder now if Lolita is a writer somewhere
scratching out how that obnoxious
	goody two shoes
	Judy Wells
always got the prizes in second grade.

She stole her Jesus
      and made a green crayon mark
      on the back of it
so even though she had to give it back
      it wasn't perfect anymore.
And Hah! Hah! Screw you
      Judy, Miss Perfect
      Goody Two Shoes.
         Screw you.

HOW I LEARNED POETRY,
THEOLOGY, AND GRAMMAR
ALL ON THE SAME DAY
IN 6TH GRADE

We kids said the Hail Mary
all in one breath
like a great run-on
sentence and of course
we knew nothing of Molly
Bloom then
It was simply
we had so many Hail Marys to say
when we said the rosary
especially in Lent
when it was down
on your knees
in the classroom
five times a day
to recite a decade
of the rosary
before we went
out to play
So one day
Sister Anne Denise
a displaced mystic
if ever there was one
and lover of the
higher things in life
(poetry and music)
but saddled with
50 sixth graders
oozing adolescence
who made her
face redder and redder
underneath her black veil

and penitential white
forehead band
took it upon herself
to teach us grammar,
theology, and poetry
all in one day.

HAIL Mary, full of GRACE!
We were to say it with excitement!
Hail! Exclamation point!
Hello! You are full of GRACE!
The Lord is with THEE;
We were to pause after THEE
and emphasize it—THEE—
Semi-colon/STOP!
Then start again
Blessed are THOU among women
Emphasize THOU—THEE, THOU
and blessed is the FRUIT
(which kind, we wondered, apples, pears, grapes)
and blessed is the FRUIT
of thy WOMB—comma—
note the comma and pause,
then say JESUS. Bow
your head on Jesus.
Jesus is in apposition to
fruit of thy womb—comma—
JESUS.

HAIL Mary, full of GRACE!
The Lord is with THEE;
blessed are THOU among women
and blessed is the FRUIT
of thy WOMB, JESUS.

We recited dutifully with
new emphasis
on all the right words
and yes it did sound better
It was poetry and grammar
and Sister Anne Denise
liked us better
when we said it this way
and then sassy Bill Dorris
or was it John Roney
had to go and ruin it
and ask about theology—
"Sister, what's a womb?"
Sister turned bright red
flustered beyond belief
—and to tell you the truth
I didn't really want to know—
but she mumbled out something like
"Why it's boys and girls, girls and boys!"
which really didn't edify
and the boys all sniggered
and that was the end of theology.

BALONEY

First, get the baloney from the refrigerator drawer.
Delicately pull the skin from around the baloney.
Savor the baloney smell. You know nothing
about how it's made from the lips and noses of pigs.

Second, get white bread from the bin—two slices.
Butter one slice of the bread.
Put the baloney on the other.

Third, turn on the oven broiler.
Place your two slices of white bread—
baloney and butter side up—under the broiler.
In several minutes the butter will melt,
                    the bread will lightly toast
and best of all, the baloney will begin to
                    sweat and curl.

Put the slices together—
                    toast both sides.
Your baloney sandwich is almost at
                    the height of its perfection.
Remove from broiler. Slather
the baloney with mayonnaise.
You are just about ready to take that
          first juicy bite of your
sweating, savory baloney sandwich
when your mother snatches it
                    from your hands.

"It's Friday!" she says.
You're crushed, you're starving.
You forgot it's Friday.
She's torturing you!

Brown bread and peanut butter loom
                    in the closet
but you know in some parts of the world
Catholics don't have this rule—why you!

Years later you become
                    a vegetarian.
NO MEAT, NO CHICKEN, NO FISH
You've gone way beyond
NO BALONEY ON FRIDAYS
and now the Catholic doctrine is dead
but you live by a new code:

As Mary Tyler Moore says,
"I never eat anything with a face."

ON GOOD DAYS, I COULD GET
KATHLEEN TO EAT MY LUNCH

"...tell me about school lunches—"
Anne Lamott, *Bird by Bird*

At St. Catherine's School
    I could not eat.
After attending Mass on First Fridays
I wasn't sure
    whether I could swallow
the sticky sweet bun
and the hot chocolate served after
    due to lump in the throat
but that wasn't the worst of it.

It was sitting
on a hard metal chair
    lined up in rows at noontime
in the great lunch hall with
    the green cement floor.
It was wadding up the remains
of my sandwich—
    even the white bread one
that had all the crusts
    cut off by my mother
and contained only a hint of butter
and maybe a smidgeon of cheese.

It was wadding up the sandwich
    carefully in the wax paper,
making a little cap of the remains
which I thought was a clever disguise
then walking bravely over to the nun
    at the door
who inspected our lunch pails

before we could leave the hall
        and go out
and play four square or basketball.

And there she was, mean old Sister,
undoing my little cap of wax paper
and finding my wadded up ball
        of white bread
and sending me back humiliated
        to my metal chair
        to sit there
till it was only me and Marleen Dunne
        sitting there alone
in the great hall, and somehow
        she managed to stuff down
whatever it was and leave
but I don't ever remember
        leaving that goddamn hall.

So people,
if you want to know
        why I'm still skinny,
You want to know the recipe,
the formula, and you
        believe in your hearts
I eat cream puffs every day
        and stuff chocolates into my mouth
and never gain an ounce
        Read this poem
and know I'm still battling
        that goddamn Sister
still battling that goddamn Sister
        Tyrant of the Lunch Pail.

LET'S TALK ABOUT THE
FUN SIDE OF CATHOLICISM
AT ST. CATHERINE'S SCHOOL

Take Father Coffey, for example.
I always thought his name was spelled
                with two e's
        until I went to Ireland.
He had a bright red balding head
        and a bum chipped tooth
and was always smiling.
Every year he went to see
        his Irish spinster aunts
                in New York,
Saw all the Broadway musicals
        and returned to St. Catherine's
                with big ideas
        for his new play,
                "The Song of Siena."
Then he'd sport flashy shirts
        and pal around with buxom
                Barbara Schultz,
P.T.A. mom and part-time producer
        of "The Song of Siena."
The whole Catholic School was in it,
        grades one to eight
and each year it got more elaborate
        until we finally had a full scale musical,
                "OKLAHOMA!"
Dennis Watson played the hero,
        Louise Koller the heroine.
I don't know how she got the part
        except she was big and well-
                developed for a kid.
She didn't have to sing.
        We lipsynched the whole play.

I had a long red skirt and bonnet
        for a square dance number,
and the guys had cowboy hats
        and drawstring ties.
We all wore bright red lipstick,
        and backstage, where we waited hours
                to go on,
we danced rock and roll
        we had learned from T.V.—
Dick Clark's American Bandstand from Philly.
        We adolescent Catholics
couldn't go to mixed parties—
        "No boys and girls together
                after 6th grade,"
but backstage Father Coffey didn't care,
        and so we whooped it up until,
"*O-O-O-O——klahoma*, where the wind comes
                sweeping down the plain,"
        and we swept out on stage
with our rickrack skirts swishing
        still thinking about Elvis,
and we weren't Judy Wells
        and Mary Jo Chantri
        and Sal Arcato
        and Philip Murphy
pipsqueaks in 7th and 8th grade—
        We were *O- K-*
                L- A- H- O- M- A !
        OKLAHOMA!

LIGHT AS THE HOLY GHOST

Father Cushnahan
who could rip through a Mass in about 20 minutes
once slid back the confessional door
and burped
in my ear.
I wonder now
whether he kept a bottle of brandy
in there to keep him company.
And was he the one
who laughed at me
when I finally dredged up
my decade old mortal sin
because I was flying overseas
and didn't want to go straight to hell
when the plane went down
over the Atlantic?
And of course the sin was nothing really,
your classic "I told a lie in confession."
I pretended I missed Mass on Sunday
when I had nothing else to say
but once you've told a lie in confession
you've really done it
because it's a sacrilege
and then you go to Communion
with a mortal sin on your soul
and you've just compounded your guilt
and then you do the same thing for 10 years
till you're a Mother Lode of mortal sins
and by God, you better confess
before you ever take an airplane trip
because you're bound to be on the doomed plane
with Satan at the helm
so even though Father Cushnahan
burped in my ear

and laughed at me
and only made me say about
5 Hail Marys
and 5 Our Fathers
for 10 years of sacrilege and guilt—
the same penance as if I confessed
I was mean to my sisters—
I sailed out of that confessional
light as the faint scent of booze
on Father Cushnahan's breath
or the Holy Ghost
ready for any flight
anyone wanted to put me on
and *this* is the power of religion
and *this* is what makes you a believer
and *this* is what makes you a poet.

BACON SANDWICHES

My father was a practical man,
painted houses in his spare time,
mowed lawns, and had a level
he measured our hair with
when he cut his three girls' bangs.
He kept the sex roles fairly straight.
He dealt with exteriors,
my mother with interiors,
except on Sunday morning
when Dad stayed in the kitchen,
and we went to Mass.

There were all kinds of things
to be done at Mass,
elbow your sister,
try not to giggle,
get the dry host down your throat
without gagging,
act holy afterwards,
laugh at Dolly Boyer in the choir
when she hit the high notes,
make sure you got your dime in the plate
and don't forget your white gloves
when you leave
even though you may have a hole
in the right one,
say hello to mom's old Uncle Frank
after Mass.

Then go down to Main Street,
buy comic books, Neccos,
try not to look at the Mickey Spillane
covers on the bad books,
then home for the best treat,

21

open up the front door,
sweet smelling smoky meat
permeates the house,
and there's Dad in the kitchen
making bacon sandwiches.

He never did quite figure out
how to do a mass feed,
so out they'd come from the broiler
one by one.
You'd have to wait your turn
and you'd almost die
as your sister or your brother
sat next to you with theirs,
wafting it before your nose.

But sometimes you were first
and you'd sink your teeth into
that cooked just right crispy bacon
and think, thanks Dad, it's O.K.
if you never go to Mass.
We don't care if you're Protestant.
Just keep on cooking
those bacon sandwiches
while we read the funnies!

THE RING

For Linda Johnson

My mother wears a large diamond ring
on her right hand,
given to her by my dad's
Uncle Frank Webb,
grandson of a Thomaston, Maine sea captain.
I have a picture
of Uncle Frank
on the deck of a ship,
no not a working sailor
he, but a well-heeled businessman
on a cruise with his wife, May,
a stout woman
in a dark dress
high buttoned shoes
large brimmed hat
a flowered parasol gripped in her two hands
like a baseball bat against the wind
leis on her bosom.
Uncle Frank lists in her direction
in a three piece white suit and shoes
a huge lei draped to his waist
cigar clenched in his teeth
Shriner's hat on his head
Staunchest Mason you could find
in all of California.

My mother tells me Masonic Frank
visited my parents'
newly built house
and returned, shocked,
to tell his sister,
my Grandma Anna,

that the Wellses had
crosses on all their doors!
(Undoubtedly my mother's influence,
a staunch Irish Catholic
who married into a Protestant family)
Yes, I guess if you look closely
at inlaid paneled doors
they do have crosses on them.
Holy Moly!
Catholic crosses
on the Wellses' doors
to ward off the Masons!

Years later, a woman I meet
who is a relative of sorts
tells me she knew my Uncle Frank
when she was a child.
He drove big cars with white sidewalls
smoked a big cigar
had a classy flat in San Francisco
with all kinds of cut glass and tapestries.
He was a real estate man
and bought Aunt May diamonds.
But Aunt May had a secret.
Aunt May was 100% Irish.
Came from a big, poor Catholic family,
alcoholic father, married a Protestant
and renounced her past
as did her sister Lucy.
And the entire Irish Catholic family
never forgave the two sisters
who broke away—
Thought they were uppity
for dumping their religion
and marrying into money.

When Aunt May died
Uncle Frank asked her sister Lucy
to live with him.
Lucy left her husband
to become Frank's "housekeeper"—
1937 or so, hush-hush scandal.
Then Uncle Frank
lover of ex-Catholic girls
Then Uncle Frank
in his Shriner's hat
Then Uncle Frank
of Holy Moly!
Catholic crosses
on the Wellses' doors
to ward off the Masons!
gave my mom,
still a Catholic girl,
one of Aunt May's
great
     big
        Masonic
            diamonds
which my mom happily flashed
on her fine
        Catholic
          hand.

AUNT ABBIE

Aunt Abbie called Uncle Frank's
first wife May
"a lady of the evening."
I guess this was a polite way
of calling her a
"You know what"—"slut"—
Let's be frank.
You've heard of Irish Aunt May before
so let's move on to Aunt Abbie.
I loved her!
She was round and cheery
and had grey braids on top of her head.
She took care of her sister
my grandma Anna
who sat solemn and silent
in her chair
when we visited.
Anna was ill with some distress
a child can never understand
so after painful minutes with her
we kids got to go into Aunt Abbie's room
and watch Gorgeous George on T.V.
Aunt Abbie would cheer on
bewigged platinum blond
down-dirty Texas wrastlin'
with the rest of us.
Then distribute silver dollars
which really won us over.
She was a Jehovah's Witness
and had a whole store of boxed slippers
in another room
for Armageddon
when it came.
She let Witnesses stay

in her rental for free
to the dismay of her son.
It was all part of Aunt Abbie's
sunny disposition towards life.
I guess she was among
the saved
and Grandma Anna, a Congregationalist,
was not.
I liked Abbie better than Anna
even though years later
Abbie's grandson, Webb,
said to me with great admiration,
Anna "was the little wren—
a very fine mind, Emily Dickinson.
She reminded me of you."

IF A BIRD ENTERS YOUR HOUSE, SOMEONE IS GOING TO DIE.

Old Irish superstition

Last summer on the Aran Islands,
on that great slab of limestone called Inishmore
we awoke to a great whirring
                    in our room.
Dale looked behind the curtains and found
a bird beating its wings between
                    curtains and window pane.
He shooshed it out.
"Don't worry," he said.
"It didn't really get into the house."
We were about to embark on a pilgrimage
to Northern Ireland,
once more in quest of my ancestors.
We searched for the dead
not knowing the dead was with us all along.

In America, on my return, my sister Nancy
said matter-of-factly on the freeway
as her husband drove us from San Francisco Airport,
"Agnes died on July 22nd while you were away."
I heard the bird beating her wings
between curtain and window pane,
the message half-delivered,
my aunt's soul
making that last, hard passage
leaving human body, reluctantly,
reluctantly, for life
on the other side.

MEMORIAL

I said she was an Irish spinster
of the highest order,
didn't date,
didn't talk about finding a man,
and didn't seem to care.
We never looked on this
as a great tragedy
when we were kids.
She had her job, her house, her trips
and her furs.
What more could a girl want?
Later, my mother said
as we got into my car,
Agnes did have a serious boyfriend once.
She did?
When? Who was it?
I had to pry the information from her
but it was like turning a stubborn can opener.
"When she was 23 or 24...
"It went on several years.
After that she wouldn't look at another man."
What happened?
"I don't want to go into it.
We had a bad year after that.
Don't mention it to the others."

But of course I did,
to my sister, Nancy, the first occasion
we were alone, an errand in her car.
"Oh, I already know about that," she said.
"Mom told me two years ago.
And then Melinda and I found that picture
in Agnes's bureau drawer."
I saw it later, a little metal-framed

photo with an advertisement on the back for
Bimbo's 365 Club, "The Home of the Girl in the Fish
    Bowl"
and on the front:
my Aunt Agnes looking sexier than I
had ever seen her in her entire life,
a young woman in a fur jacket
her head tossed back
red lipstick framing a huge smile
sheer delight on her face
a saucy black hat tipped on her head
eyes that said, "I'm in love"
and next to her

a hole in the picture
a certain someone excised
from the shot with a razor blade.
The only equivalent I could think of
was Bridget's ex, Tony,
who, years ago, had a photo of himself
on his mantle
with Bridget whited out
after she left him for Tunis.
My aunt's tool was more vicious,
a razor blade.
I'll never know who was in that blank
unless my mother will tell.

There's a second photo of my aunt in another
little metal frame.
This one with the Golden Gate Exposition on the back.
She looks ten years older
the same bright red lipstick
but the smile is gone
no gleam in her eye, laugh on her face.
She wears perfunctory clothes:

a cloth coat
a dress with a white collar
a black hat centered on her head
with a little white bow.
She's settled into a life without ecstasy
as most people do.
I do not blame her
but Christ, I'd like to
wring that bastard's neck
who broke her pretty red heart in two
and set her
                against herself.

THROW AWAY EVERYTHING

For Agnes L. Smith
1905-1993

If you don't
when you are dead
your relatives will see
   EVERYTHING
Your tax bill from 1978
Your 30 year old Kotex
Your dresses stained
with your dinners
Your school pictures
when you were cute
Samples of your handwriting
when you were 13
Literature from all the causes you
foolishly or wisely gave money to
All the old Kleenexes
you kept in your pockets
All the coins you
stashed in your drawers
Your old mink hat and stole
Your still stylish beaver
jacket you could never
now wear in San Francisco
The half dozen pair of gloves
you bought and never wore
The score of straw purses
you stashed in your closets
The odd pieces of silverware you
collected over the years
which you thought your helper stole
Your old Christmas cards
from the last 20 years

Everything, everything
will be there, somewhere
Even the pearl ring
you lost in your house
It will turn up somewhere
in the bathroom
or in the corner of the basement
under a pile of dirt
Someone will unearth this gem
and say finally:

This was my aunt
A woman who knitted
Knit one, purl two
Knit one, purl two
Throw away the yellow wool
The grey wool
The half-knitted dress
Throw away the needles
Knit one, purl two
This was my aunt
A girl once
A child once
who cried out
"Mama, Mama,"
before she died
Knit one, purl two
She was once a young girl
This knit one, purl two
This pearl of a girl, my aunt.

WAKING THE DEAD

ADRIFT

An American has a life of schedules:
E-mail, meetings, appointments
for students, car, hair, teeth,
skin and her unseen interior.
Then she has this dream:
She steps on a wooden pier/bridge
      over a river
and the planks cut loose
and she with them.
She thought she was going
      to cross the river
as she saw others do
but no, and so she enjoys herself
until she realizes, "I'm just
      tossing down the river"
and she gets off at the next pier.

She awakes, remembers the Irish
voyager stories:
A criminal or hero is set adrift
      in a boat
like the baby in *The Secret of Roan Inish*
with the huge mop of dark hair.
The hero drifts with no oars
to an island of shouting birds,
one of giant ants,
another of all women,
places you would only find
as the Indian story goes, after
      rowing upstream
      rowing upstream
and you finally raise your oars
      and sing!

Drift, drift
so un-American
      Control your life!
      Control your destiny!
Drift, drift
like the child in the sea cradle
with the black mop of hair.
Drift, drift
One day you'll touch your island
of glass, of fire, of giant ants
      on a river of honey.
Drift, drift
Daughter of wheat
Son of milk
adrift in a big bowl of cream.
      Spoons, please!
      Oars, please!
     Sing!

A RIVER RUNS
THROUGH MY NECKLACE
A RIVER RUNS
THROUGH MY HEAD

The Irish say
if you live by a river
you'll hear the voices in the river
which will drive
        you
           crazy

A river runs through my necklace
A river runs through my head

The Irish say
on St. Patrick's day
the stones turn over
in the river
and the cold
goes out of winter

A river runs through my necklace
A river runs through my head

I wonder what
the stones say
when they turn over
Enough of this cold, they say?
Let's warm our backsides
in the sun
Let's change the currents
Let warmth permeate
even stone

Or do they whisper other strange things
about who your mother is
or the time you made
love to the stars
or the scream
you store under your bed

A river runs through my necklace
A river runs through my head

The Irish say
if you live by a river
you'll hear the voices in the river
which will drive
         you
             crazy

WHAT WE FORGOT

"Beware, beware, Mac Conglinne,
lest the gravy drown thee!"
The Vision of Mac Conglinne
12th century

*For 4th and 5th generation
Irish-Americans*

We forgot our language
We forgot the land we came from
      had rolling green hills
We forgot our songs
We forgot our stories
We forgot we were cattle people
We forgot our voyage tales
      where the West didn't mean
            only Death
      where the West meant
         Tir na n'Og
    The Land of Youth
      where there was no decay
We forgot the islands of women
The land in the sea
      surrounded by sea horses
We forgot the sea
      was a plain of red flowers
which Manannan mac Lir
      thundered through in his chariot

We forgot we ever had a vision
      of a silly land of surfeit
      where we rowed on a lake of milk
         skimming cream
      where castles were made of
         butter and lard
    and our palisades, of bacon

We forgot we had cheese gates
          and cheese stepping stones
and a voracious demon who slipped
                    inside our mouths
          in an apple
whom a cleric called Mac Conglinne
          enticed from our king's gullet
by enumerating
          all the things
the demon liked to eat—
          curds and whey
          and milk and lard
          and bacon and mutton
          and buttered rolls and mead
until the demon couldn't stand
          it anymore and leaped
                    from the king's throat
and there were lands
          where you could eat a bird's egg
                    and then sprout feathers
and lands where the fragrance of
          crimson trees satisfied your hunger
and lands where multi-colored birds
          blue, crimson, and green
                    sat three in a row
          and sang away your grief
and Yeats tried to tell us
          but only a little

And we tried to forget in America
          We wanted real bacon
                    in our bellies
          and we wanted shoes
          and then we wanted fancy red-flowered hats
          and we wanted an education
so we could become lawyers,

and nurses and school teachers
so we would not have to be domestics
            and serve roasted birds
to "our betters" who would never sprout
                              feathers

Never fly as we did
            with the knowledge of our tales
                        over seas of red flowers
                        over seas of red flowers
We forgot, we forgot our tales
            and remembered only
                        dark seas
                        and coffin ships
We forgot our seas of red flowers
            and Manannan mac Lir on his steed
                        galloping to meet us
            where we were
                        Queen of the island
                                    with 17 daughters
                        Queen of the island
                                    with 17 daughters

THE CLIFFMAN

(a man is speaking)

"This bizarre hunt is of unknown
but certainly ancient origin."
Tim Robinson, *Stones of Aran*

I did it for the first time
    when I was 15 years old.
I can say it now—
We humans are a brutal force
    in the universe
but I was young then, nimble,
    and innocent.
My father and his friends, drunk
    on poteen,
tied the rope around my waist
and lowered me down the cliff.
My legs banged against the jagged rock.
My head, nearly, but I used a stick
    to keep my distance.
I was terrified. It was a cold
    moonless night,
dry, but sweat soaked my vest.
It was an eternity before my feet
    touched the ledge.
"Are ye all right now?"
    the men called down.
I wanted nothing more than to scream
"No! Haul me back up, Da!"
but I groaned an "Aye."
I was on the narrow ledge
on all fours, like a dog.
My hands trembled as I unloosened
    the rope from my waist.
They hauled the rope back up.

"We'll be back at dawn, Paddy,"
      they yelled.
I felt sick, nauseous, knowing
      a few feet away
I could plunge 100 feet down into the sea.
The birds were nesting on the ledges.
My job—bring them back up the cliff—
for food and feathers for the pillows
      of Galway.
I crept on all fours down the ledge.
The first bird was the hardest.
I wrapped one arm around it,
kneeling now—it struggled a bit—
and with my right hand I wrenched its neck.
I was surprised how easy it was
and how little I cared.
I pushed this bird forward on the ledge
so as not to startle the others.
They trusted me, the fools.
I had only one goal—
kill as many birds as possible.
At first I wondered how I would do it,
but by the twentieth bird I lost count.
I began to enjoy the feel of feathers under my fingers,
the little sounds the bones made as they failed.
My mastery in the air.
I worked and worked for hours
until a bleak dawn spread over the water.
I looked down, my head reeling.
I trailed behind me 12 score birds on a line.
My fisher's catch of the night.
"Sing out, Paddy. Where are ye?"
came the morning's feeble call.
I had to crawl back over my string
      of dead birds.

Several hundred glassy eyes
        stared up at me
in the half light. It was eerie.
I lay over the cliff and spilled my guts
        into the sea.
I was the new cliffman of my village.
They would call me a man now.
They hurled the rope down from above.
It nearly hit my head.
"Was it a good night, Paddy?"
"Aye, Da, a good night," I said
but for the love of God
as they hauled me back up the cliff
        with my catch,
I wished myself off this brutal island,
cutting turf with a clean spade—
and at night sleeping
        on a feather bed
made from some other cliffman's catch.

WARP SPASM

Was it a good thing Ireland
                was Christianized in the fifth century?
Did the Celts really hang heads from their belts?
Embed skulls in their gates?
Sit with their knee over a freshly hacked head,
holding their antagonist's power as their own?

Jesus had to be a gentler force,
but I've heard this argument before.
Why then does the pope have Swiss guards?

Still when your hero is Cuchulainn,
a superboy who makes our t.v. violence
                look like pablum,
Who has a warp spasm instead
                of a fit of anger,
Can leap fords in a single bound,
Has a giant ejaculation of violence,
and then reports he'll be your guard dog,
I'd say Ireland was ripe for sects
                of men and women
who did not want warp spasms
                to be their lot in life.
Or cattle raids—why cling to cows
when you could illuminate great books
and use the spirals of the Goddess,
Those great wavy lines of water-lacing
                to praise the Lord,
putting axe, sword, and shield
                to rest.

Yes, I would have joined the Celtic monks.
I've read women were allowed early on,

Remnants of their rights
        under Brehon Law,
Remnants of their rights
        under the Goddess Brigit,
Remnants of their rights
        under the Triple Goddess.
Yes, I would have gone to Skellig Michael,
        island on the high seas,
Let a petrel hatch in my hand
though it take two centuries.
Would have sat in a stone beehive hut
built with my own hands,
watched the Big Dipper cup the sky,
the Vikings hurl by in their long boats.

I would have had my paints in my hut
as I was writing my own illuminated manuscript,
not the famous gospel books
        the Irish hold today,
but my own bird manuscript.
I still believed in augury—
        divination by the birds.
I said my prayers when a certain
        bird's egg was hatched,
not when the abbot rang a brass bell.
I lived by the cracks of eggs,
By the peeps of newly hatched chicks,
By their first struggle to fly,
        their cries for food.
We had one gold crucifix
Michael brought from Kilmalkedar—
our only sign of splendor on the island.
All the rest from God.

I should not say God—only.
I still believed in Lugh, pulling his
                chariot across the sky.
I still believed in Brigit
who guided my pen as I wrote
                my book of birds.
I still knew if I saw
                a puffin born with two heads
I would have to leave the island forever
and burn the entwined ravings of my pen.
They were the only colors on my island,
The only brilliant reds and bright greens.
The rest was stone, the seeds of stars,
steps between water and heaven—
hermitage of my heart
gardens of bliss
bouquets of prayers
days of penance
curls of incense
stays of solitude
My heart on fire
My hands for Christ
My eyes for Mary
My love for all mysteries
of earth, water, fire, and air.

BLACK IRISH

On May 28, 1588, 130 ships with
more that 30,000 men set sail
from Lisbon. Two thirds of the
Spanish Armada were wrecked as
storms defeated them.

We found him on the rocks,
me brother and me.
Looked almost drowned to death
but I put me hand to his chest
and he was breathing all right.
I got me brother
to load him up on our cart
and take him back into the hills
to our hut.
We didn't treat him
like the others did—strip
the coins from his pockets.
Not that this one had any coins.
He was dressed all in red
like them rowers
on the great Spanish ships.
Imagine a whole row of them
in those bright red outfits,
rowing like eejits across the seas
to fight the English.
One-eyed Jack here last night
told us how the English hanged
some of them Spanish sailors
but I kept mine hid.
Now I know our storytellers
are going to tell you
them Spanish sailors are how
we come by all our "Black Irish"
but I want to set the record straight.

That Spanish sailor we plucked
from the rocks
couldn't have knocked up a thing
the condition he was in.
He was near to his death
with fever and chill.
We put him in the sweat hut
for three days straight
and finally gave him a shot
of poteen.
That brought him round.
He couldn't a been more
than a score and two.
I was thirty and to tell you the truth
that's why me brother
lugged him all the way up
to our hut.
All the young men in our village
either left or married up
for a wee bit of land
so this sailor boy, yes,
I had me eye on him.
Looked so fine
in that bright red suit.
Then, when I undressed him,
Muscles you couldn't believe
from all that rowing.
Yes, I wanted him but
that floppy little piece
below his waist didn't rise
for a long time.
Of course, he couldn't speak a lick
of Irish
nor I Spanish
but when he finally came around
and had eaten potatoes and buttermilk

for three days straight
as if he'd never had a decent
meal in his life
and I had me back to him
scraping out the pots
he reached around me and put
his dark hand
on me breast.
We tumbled down right there
on the earthen floor
and went at it
like animals.
Nine months later
Tommy was born,
hair black as a moonless night
but fair like me.
That Spanish sailor
still lives with me.
Neighbors are used to Carlos by now.
He even knows some Irish.
I patched up that little red suit
he came to me in.
Just feeling it excites me some.
There'll be more
little black-haired babies to come,
but I have to tell you
there's another story going round
about Carlos and me—
the one where the day of the wreck
he turned right over on the beach—
looked at me
and his cock was straight up.
I could see the bulge in his pants,
and he took me right there on the beach
as did all them Spanish sailors
with me sisters

like they was horny as hell
even if they were near drowned.
Well, it's not true!
Took more like seven days
for us women
to bring those men around.
It's me story
and I'm sticking to it.

WAKING THE DEAD / PEIG'S FUNERAL

"Few people nowadays, even in
Ireland, are aware that the old
horse-play (of the Irish wakes)
included some quite elaborate
mimed dramas, reminiscent of
fertility ritual."
                    Vivian Mercier
                    The Irish Comic Tradition

Shhhh.... Shhhh....
I'm going to let you in on
        a little Irish secret.
They say we're sexually repressed.
        Do you believe it?
See this potato?
They say it was because of this potato
        we went from 5 million population
                in 1801 in Ireland
        to over 8 million
                in the next 40 years!
Did you ever see a potato turn
        into a baby?
                        Did you?
                Not I.
And here's another little Irish secret.

At our Irish wakes
        we played games you wouldn't believe.
We had a mock priest
who wore a rosary of potatoes.
He sprinkled us couples with water
        and tucked us into a corner
murmuring "Crescite et multiplicamini!"
        "Increase and multiply!"
We played Making the Ship—
        erecting the mast—if you get my gist.

Then there was Selling the Pig
        Turning the Spit
        and Performing Tricks on the Corpse.
We even had one game where our men stripped
        down naked
        and faced us women.

Sure the body was laid out
        in front of us.
We know the body.
That's why I am.
        Came out of old Peig's body.
        Course she was young Peig then.
She played these games herself.
Did you ever make love
        the night someone died
        and you cut loose like you never did before
and it was the best sex you ever had?

Well, I can tell you after playing
        all those wake games,
                We were awake.
Our bodies were trembling to be laid,
        and we made love soon after
                with our partners
and it was sacred sex by then,
        after all that laughing
        and all that keening
        and all that playing.
It was sacred sex by then.

And old Peig sailed out
        on her coffin ship
                to all those Western lands
she had to travel to—
        and we in her wake—

laughing, Making the Ship,
sailing we don't know where.
All we know is there'll be more
than the usual number of births
      on the island
nine months after our funferall—
      I mean—our funeral—
and some of them
are sure to be called her name—
               Peig.

THE ANCESTORS DANCE

For all the dead of
The Great Hunger, 1845-49,
and for two bands:
Kíla and Dead Can Dance

The shaman plays the bodhrán
and the ancestors dance.
Yes, the dead can dance.
The shaman plays the bodhrán
and the ancestors sing.
Yes, the dead can sing.

The shaman plays the bodhrán
and the famine dead
rise from their graves
and sing away their grief.
And they eat.
Yes, the eat their fill of meat
and they eat their fill of cheese
and they eat their fill of plump brown potatoes.
Yes, the dead can eat
while the shaman plays the bodhrán.

Then they dance.
Then they dance away their grief
and all the dead children
from the coffin ships
rise from the Atlantic
with seaweed in their hair
and form a chain with their hands
across the sea.

And they dance.
Yes, the dead can dance.
And they sing.

Yes, the dead can sing
away your grief.

And they can play.
And they can play
percussion on a goat skin drum
with their bones
till the whole world's
dancing with the dead.
Yes, the dead can dance
and they can sing
and what they sing is—

Yes, you will join us.
One day you will join us
and you'll sing
and you'll dance
to the bodhrán
of the stars
to the bodhrán
of the spheres
to the bodhrán
of the planets
and the moon
and the sun.

Yes, you'll dance
to the bodhrán of the moon
for the dead can dance.

THE NORTH

"The great Hugh O'Neill of Tyrone
was crowned in 1593 on Tullaghoge hill.
It was the headquarters
of the O'Hagans,
chief justices of Ireland,
who performed the coronations
of the O'Neill kings
from the 12th to 17th century."
            Northern Ireland Information Bulletin

In the late 20th century
Dale and I booked rooms
with Mrs. Margaret O'Hagan
in County Tyrone, Northern Ireland.
I had wanted my ancestors
to be from the Republic, the South.
But no, they were all from the North.
Mrs. O'Hagan
could have been my aunt
by another name.
I sat in her living room
huddled by her fake fireplace—
an electric heater
covered with plastic
red and orange coals
with a light underneath.
Horses charged through the room
from the blue rug which hung on the wall.
Twin porcelain dogs sat on the mantle
and a peasant girl with a Japanese umbrella
stood in the corner.
Mrs. O'Hagan, small, permed, and suspicious
sat amongst this kitsch
on a brown and yellow flowered couch.
I tried to extract dry towels from her
in a roundabout way.

"Are the damp towels in the bathroom ours?" I asked.
"You can use them if you want," she said.
Foiled, we went to our room. It was moldy and damp
with the Blessed Virgin over our bed.
There was a grey wig
on top of our wardrobe
a cowboy hat
and tucked in a corner, hidden,
The Proclamation of the Irish Republic in a frame.

When I finally asked Mrs. O'Hagan again for the
        towels,
she had a sly look on her face,
cunning you might say.
"Oh, do you really think they used them?" she said.
"They" being three British lads in their 20s
one with a long blond pony tail
and one German girl with a bizarre shaved head
with a mop on top.
"Well of course they used them!
They've been in that bathroom for hours."
I thought maybe she couldn't afford more towels,
but then she opened a closet stuffed with linens
and extracted two clean towels
we should have gotten straight off.
Mr. O'Hagan appeared out of nowhere,
unshaved,
semi-toothless,
an older man, still stocky and friendly.
He kept urging us to make ourselves at home
but we couldn't.
We both had the flu.
The damp moldy room wouldn't do.
We almost left
but it was too much trouble.
The rain came down,

and Northern Ireland was bleak as its politics.
"You'd think I was a British spy
the length of time it took to get a dry towel,"
I complained to Dale.
The next morning Mr. O'Hagan was shaved,
his hair slicked back.
He was going to Newry, a "border town"
with his daughter.
She sang traditional and country music.
They would raise a few jars today.

Yesterday when we told him
we didn't have a car,
he said we were "on shank's mare"
and I said yes!
That's what my mother always said
when we had to walk.
Mr. O'Hagan said he knew then
I had some Irish in me
and Dale kept saying in private
"You're home!"
but it made me mad.
I didn't like these people
who wouldn't give me towels, didn't shave,
kept a frigid house full of Irish kitsch.
Red pampas grass in vases,
A pendulum clock that ticked me off!
The morning we were about to leave
I picked up a miniature Irish thatched cottage,
"Ceis Fada" in Gaelic, #93, was over the door.
Mr. O'Hagan was all good cheer.
"That was made by a prisoner at Long Kesh" he said.
"We know lots of people in Long Kesh,
one coming out after 25 years,"
and he showed us a little Irish harp
a prisoner made out of matchsticks.

61

And I thought how ironic.
These men are put in jail for crimes
against Protestants and Brits,
and they make Irish crafts in their cells.
Then Mr. O'Hagan showed me a picture of a stout lad
in a red sweater,
one of his relatives.
This man, age 22, and two others
were shot to death a few miles
down the road.
From that day, the O'Hagans
were subject to raids.
A wagon drives up, the police come in,
close all the curtains,
put them in two different rooms,
search though all the cupboards,
throwing everything on the floor.
What are they looking for? I ask.
"That's the point," says Mr. O'Hagan.
"We wouldn't be stupid enough to hide
anything here if we did have something!"
"It's just harassment," I said.
"They get set on some people," said Mr. O'Hagan.
"You must have been scared," I said.
"You can't live here if you're scared,"
said Mrs. O'Hagan.
"You'd be gone."
We were, shortly
but returned to America with a sympathetic tale—
two old people, civil rights violated,
suffering raids in their own home.

Five months later,
I read a piece in the San Francisco *Chronicle*
about Northern Ireland.
The name jumped out:

Felim O'Hagan is one of the most
"famous inhabitants of Long Kesh," the article says.
"Convicted of killing two policemen
in an IRA assault in 1976,
when he was 21, he is 17 years
into a 175 year sentence."
One of his cousins states proudly,
"For six generations, there has never
been a time when the men
of our family have not been
in prison or on the run."

Name: O'Hagan. Chief Justices of Ireland for five
        centuries.
Name: O'Hagan. Chief prisoners of Northern Ireland
        in the 20th century.

Irishmen and Irishwomen:

        In the name of God
        and of the dead generations
        from which she receives her old tradition of
            nationhood,
        Ireland, through us, summons her children
        to her flag and strikes for her freedom.

Irishmen and Irishwomen:

        When will the bloodletting stop?

December 3, 1993
First day of the initial negotiations between the British
and Irish for peace in Northern Ireland.

"RAISE YOUR JAR AT BIDDY'S BAR," SAID BRIAN, THE BUS DRIVER.

St. Columbcille, an outlaw saint
banished from Ireland for taking
up arms, founded a monastery in
Iona, Scotland. On one occasion,
he returned to save Ireland's order
of feisty bards at the convention
at Drumceatt.

For Sarah Fike

I studied Biddy's Bar
while Dale made the call.
It was a two story affair,
Two chimneys
Two doors
and lace curtains all around.
"Bridget" was neatly lettered over one door.
"McShane" over the other,
and at one end of the house
lettered in black and blue
THE
CROSS   ROADS
BAR
with a church pew underneath it.
"No dice," said Dale.
"Both Gillespie cabs are out."
"I'll ask in the bar" I said.
"Sarah said she ended up
in somebody's kid's bed when she was here."
I entered the "Bridget" door
and found myself in a dark hole.
There was a line of old men
on the back wall
and a line of young ones at the bar.
"Can anyone take us to the Glencolumbcille Hotel?"

I asked. No, said the female barkeep,
she didn't know anyone
who could take us out.
Sorry.
"What!" I thought.
Sarah said all our problems would be solved in the bar.
I slunk out amidst the stares of the old men
and spotted my young friend from the bus
still hovering round the phone booth outside.
"We can't get a ride," I said.
She put her head together with another woman.
"Maybe Barry at the shop or Colum.
Go ask them for Colum's phone number.
He's the only one who could take you."
Barry couldn't do it. He had a grocery run to make,
but we got Colum's number.
I heard Dale through the glass door
of the phone booth
explaining about the two Gillespies
and could he...
Eureka!
A car soon drove up.
We looked in.
An older man stared at us.
Dale stuck out his hand
with no result
while I stared in horror
at the man's huge lower lip.
A crusty, bloody mass of blisters.
O my God, I thought.
The only man who'd take us to
the Glencolumbcille Hotel is a leper.
It was as if the town sent out
a ghoul to greet us.
A scene out of a horror movie.
And what next—

the axe in your back?
Not exactly fair, I thought.
I get fever blisters too.
We got in.
I couldn't get over Dale's gesture
offering his hand to an Irish stranger
and the Irish stranger's coldness
as he clung to the steering wheel,
Dale's hand invisible to him.
The man soon began to chat
in a soft voice.
"I've been out fishing for five days
on the bay," he said
as we headed out of town.
"That's how I got me lip."
"The sun?" I asked, knowing
that's how mine are triggered,
but I felt like a fool.
The sun did not come out in the north of Ireland
in the summer of 1993.
"The salt" he said.
I winced.
We drove on past Father McDyer's Folk Park—
thatched cottages built to attract
tourists like us to this remote
corner of Donegal.
The guide books considered Father McDyer a saint.
"Did you know him?" I asked.
"Aye," he said.
"He never paid for a thing!"
Another little chill went through me.
The rain came down in fits.
The slate grey bay was spectacular
and Colum told us we'd be
all right in the Glencolumbcille Hotel.
"It was a former coast guard station."

Dale asked how much we owed him.
"I'll give you the cheap rate," he said.
"Five punts." Dale gave him six
for the two mile jaunt,
and he reached out his hand this time.
The town was small
but we never saw Colum again.

I WANT MY PUD!

Mainister House
means Monastery House
in Irish but now
it's a gourmet vegetarian youth hostel
on Inishmore
run by Joël d'Anjou,
a small black man
with slicked back hair,
dark glasses on his head,
white jeans and a black and white
striped shirt. I've heard
he speaks seven languages.
I've heard he was adopted
by Scots-Presbyterians, but
most of all, I've heard
he's mysterious, and no one knows
where he's from.

                The hostel
dining room is set
with blue and white napkins
tucked into wine glasses.
It's bursting with travelers and kids
and a bulky older couple with a huge wine bottle.
Joël d'Anjou hates dining rooms
where you can only hear
the clicking of knives and forks
so he sets us in clusters
to see what will happen.
There's a table of Irish Clanceys
who don't know each other
and a table of "us":
two blond Danish women in their thirties,
Dale who passes for Scandinavian or German,

68

a stout woman with a big bosom and ruddy
    complexion,
an English-looking older gent
with even ruddier bent,
and me, a quarter Irish.

"I've been coming to this island for 30 years,"
announces the Bosom,
declaring herself Queen of our table.
I discreetly inquire about Joël d'Anjou,
but she's terse.
"His parents are from Edinburgh.
He went to Eaton and Oxford.
He ran a cafe in town,
and was asked to be chef at the hostel."
Her companion is hostile:
"He's got a sun tan!"
"I don't like that!" she replies.
"He was born with that skin."

The ruddy man sips his wine,
says he was born in Dublin,
raised in the West of Ireland,
but by all rights, he is from Dublin!
"Just because you were born in a stable
doesn't mean you're an ass!" she quips.
I laugh mightily, and the Queen is pleased,
but, of course, I know he's not an ass—
He's an asshole!

"The only Protestant Church on Inishmore
doesn't have a roof over it!" announces the Queen,
hinting the asshole should pay for the roof.
"There's a task for you," I say to the ruddy man.
"Go around with a donation box."
"Oh, he wouldn't do that!" she replies.

"He'd delegate it!" I understood
I had met the Anglo-Irish.

While we're conversing, the Clanceys
attack Joël's veggie table first,
make off with all the asparagus,
then the green beans. We pounce on
the remains of the pasta and fish sauce
and tossed green salad.
To compensate for the Clancey gap,
Joël brings out a huge bowl
of potatoes and a fruit compote,
saying, "Thirds are O.K.,"
and we bolt to the table.

The asshole, a bachelor in his fifties,
complains about the lack of divorce in Ireland.
At a recent dinner party of 24 in Dublin,
only five people were happy,
two couples and him.
Everyone else was separated.
He seemed to be eying
the more outgoing Danish blond
as a potential drinking partner
at Joe Watty's after supper,
but he had gone way beyond
a rapport with women.
"I WANT MY PUD!" he proclaimed.

"Don't call it a pud. Call it a sweet, a dessert!
Not pudding!" replied the Queen.
"I have a sweet tooth!" pouted the asshole.
"Ask for a dessert," said the Queen.
The asshole beckoned the young Irish waiter
and asked whether he could have a sweet.
"I'll bring you the menu," said the waiter.

The two Danes, Dale and I
politely waited with the asshole.
The Clanceys all left, and the help
rattled all around us.
"CHRISTINA, is it?" said the Queen
to the waitress.
"I think I still am," she replied
and sped off.

Finally, Joël d'Anjou came by
with his mysterious eyes
that looked in two directions.
"Where's the dessert the waiter
promised him?" demanded the Queen.
"Dessert?" said Joël, rolling his eyes.
"Oh, he was just joking."
"Come, make him apologize," demanded the Queen.
We were all laughing by now, except
of course, the asshole.
          "I WANT MY PUD!"

ANTIDOTE

Every ethnic culture
needs its antidote.
That's why Limerick B & B owner Mrs. Burke
boasted of going to the Canary islands every winter.
That's why Mr. Larry Bogan,
mild-mannered accountant from Galway,
impersonates Elvis Presley
in his favorite pub.
It's the steamy South he wants.
That's why I
after three summers in Ireland
the last one in Glencolumbcille
where the rain came down in sheets
and in Omagh, County Tyrone,
sleeping in damp sheets, o my,
when not even defying
the Blessed Virgin
over our bed
could keep us warm,
That's why I
went to Hawaii last summer
where warm turquoise waters
curled around my loins
and Hawaiian dancers reminded us
pelvises were made to move
and hips to sway
and not be locked in place
doing "makety uppity" Irish dances
as Irish poet Nuala Ní Dhomhnaill calls them.
That's why I
went to Hawaii last summer
so the sun could
penetrate my bones
and I could scoop

sweet, succulent orange flesh from the papaya
instead of opting for a baked potato
one more time
so I could drink the antidote
of my own green culture
and quench my thirst for wild

wild ginger!

MRS. JENSEN, MRS. JENSEN, WHICH WAY WERE YOU LOOKING WHEN THE SINK WAS OVERFLOWING?

In Ireland, when you're
traveling as a couple,
it's best to be a Mrs.
even if you're not.

Of course it had to be in Dublin
in our favorite B & B
a beautiful Victorian house with a yellow door
and yellow roses out front
on a most convenient busline
and a motherly Mrs. O'Donoghue
with yellow hair
and stout eyebrows

And the mere thought of her voice
reduces me to a naughty ten year old
or sometimes a babbling two year old
Mrs. Jensen, Mrs. Jensen,
which way were you looking
when the sink was overflowing

And I had only wanted to wash my blue comb
so I put it in the basin to soak
Then turned on the shower
to soak myself for a good while
after a five hour bus trip
from the very northwest tip
of Ireland, from a speck
called Glencolumbcille
to clear across Ireland
to Dublin

We had to sit
in the back of the bus
and I rather bounced
clear across Ireland
on McGeehan's bus—
they had a deal
with the Brits
they could short cut
through the North
if they wouldn't stop

So we barrelled straight through
to Cavan—
where everyone ran to
the bathrooms—
and then an Irish woman
and I began to chat
at the back of the bus

Her father was 82 years old
a weaver for 60 years in Donegal
She was the youngest of nine children
lived in England, no work
for her in Donegal
No, she didn't know Gaelic
and when I asked her what she said
when asked what part of Ireland
she came from
she said "the South"
but her sister said "the North"
and sometimes she said "the border"
The dilemma of Donegal

And all this while we jostled
in the back of the bus

I asked her if she'd ever been to New Grange
She'd never heard of Ireland's most sacred site
and I was almost embarrassed to tell her
and all this was running through my head
in the shower
I was still riding on McGeehen's bus
in the shower

So I wasn't thinking **SINK** or **BLUE COMB**
after 15 minutes in that shower
But when I got out
I was thinking **SINK** and **BLUE COMB**
and how the hell can I mop up
all this water

And then I had to confess the mess to Mom
    O'Donoghue
and then she said the rug
would have to be replaced, of course
and then she noticed the wet plaster
in her apartment down below
and then Dale had to go down there
and give her our address in Berkeley
and tell her he'd pay the deductible
on her insurance

And then she said,
Mrs. Jensen, I'd just like to know
which way you were looking
when the sink was overflowing

And the next morning
I nearly choked on my full Irish breakfast
I was so humiliated
and we dared not stay another day
Our bags were packed

and then she said, "You will come back, Mr. Jensen"
in that tone "if you dare"

And that is why I haven't been back
                              to Ireland

HUNGER

For Bridget Connelly
and her father

Did you see it there
in Minnesota, sister,
Hunger?
A hard, cold knot
in your stomach
those cold winter nights?
No?
Well, maybe your ancestors
saw it then,
a thin gruel
for their evening meal
and then to bed
dizzy from their fast.
You conjure up
a cozy kitchen,
three fresh baked pies
sitting on the table.
The sons come in
with apples on their cheeks
and wolf down mom's hot stew.
They don't remember either.
But one man did,
a lean, hard man
who believed you too
could move the earth.
A man with a brown felt hat
who died when he was forty-two,
looking at the land, they say,
with gaunt blue eyes.

FEASTDAY OF THE
BLESSED VIRGIN MARY
AT ST. MARY'S COLLEGE

"...in one place the people
are starving but wonderfully
attractive and charming...."
John Millington Synge

An odd man with silver hair
sat two pews up.
He looked like Anthony Perkins
with his handsome, gaunt face
and pronounced cheekbones.
He held himself
hands clutching his elbows.

When the priest came to the consecration,
the most sacred part of the Mass,
the odd man held his hands
delicately in front of him
in the exact way the priest held his,
and when the priest genuflected,
the odd man bowed his head
as if he were saying the Mass himself.
I could almost see the chords
moving in his throat.
I thought he was an ex-priest
or a priest with AIDS.
It happens, we know.

He took communion with the rest,
bread in his mouth,
drank from the wine cup,
and I noticed his shoes were untied.
When we said "Peace be with you"
to our neighbor,

82

we all shook hands with him,
and he smiled
a handsome high cheekbone smile
but still, I did not think him well.

Later we saw him
at Brother Mel's picnic
where the food was copious.
The potato salad multiplied
as did the slices of chicken
baked beans and deviled eggs.
There was wine and pop
and watermelon and potato chips,
and I saw the odd man with the silver hair
by himself
with a plastic bag from Safeway,
gathering up silverware and food
and it all went into his plastic bag.

He gathered quite a lot
and sat with no one
and then he disappeared.
And then it struck me
something Bridget had said
about Synge
who admired the gaunt faces
of the Connemarans
of Western Ireland.
"They were starving," she said,
"and he thought them beautiful."

August 15, 1995

RAINY DAY WOMAN

If I saw myself walking
in the stream of history
If I saw myself walking
in the stream of history
Where would I be?
If I raised myself
over my self in my red coat
If I raised myself
over my self in my red raincoat
Where would I be?

I'd be walking in the 20th century
toward the 21st
I'd be walking to Benilde Hall
to my job as an Academic Counselor
at St. Mary's College

And in me is a Brother
walking to his dorm in Benilde Hall
and in me is a Mexican nun
walking in a cloistered garden
and in me is a bare strip of land
and in me is a deer
running from a hunter
and in me is an Indian
seeking a winter meal
and in me is a marsh
and in me is an earthquake
and in me is a woman walking
in a red raincoat
over a Catholic campus

And in me is a woman wondering
whether I am marching

in the stream of history
or away from it
Whether I am an anachronism
or exemplar of the 21st century
a seer or sample
of what's to come
a childless woman
to be forgotten
or avatar
to be remembered

Will the deer in me, turtle,
rabbit and all things small
symbolize my demise or triumph?
Will the meditator arise,
the vegetarian triumph
or will the carnivore
push into the 21st century
        Incarnate
           and
destroy the White Deer?

I WENT TO HOLY COMMUNION
FOR THE FIRST TIME IN 25 YEARS

I went to Holy Communion
for the first time in 25 years
            at St. Mary's Chapel.
        I felt nothing,
except perhaps the same dryness
            in my throat
I felt at my first communion
            when I was seven years old.
I did not drink from the new innovation,
the wine cup, though I know now
                    why others do.

A few weeks later
            I drove onto St. Mary's campus
and saw a great bird sitting atop
            a tall pine tree.
Its wings were spread and
                        it was perfectly still.
I stepped on the brakes and
            stared at the great bird,
and the Holy Ghost fluttered within me
                    ever so lightly,
and I was filled with excitement.

A car was behind me
            so I drove on.
I thought perhaps the bird brother
            at St. Mary's
had set a decoy atop the tree
                    to attract other birds,
        or the students had set up
a prank mascot in front of the gym.

And I just had to go back
                    after I parked.
When I returned, the great bird—
            my Holy Ghost—was gone
and a skulking turkey vulture
            huddled on a branch below.

Recently a priest told me
            he dreamed a great woodpecker
was pecking on a vein
                        in his neck.
      It hammered and hammered.
He awoke, wrenching the bird away,
            felt substance in his hands.
He enacted this dream
            over and over,
And I thought again of the Holy Ghost
            pecking at his chosen ones
leaving others
                    free.

MY SPIRITUAL LIFE

Brother Camillus gave us
    an inspiring Easter talk—
How he once left the brotherhood
    filled with passion for a woman
        and raging against God
until he was stopped one day
    by a vision.
"I saw Christ carrying his crucifix,
    streams of blood carved his cheeks.
He said to me, 'I have done all this.
    What have you done?'"
And Camillus returned to his faith,
      his calling,
which magnified before our little group
    of meditators.
He then played for us a tape
    of joyful, spiritual music,
then a Baroque adagio for strings
    and an image rose before me—
What was it? The sacred heart?
    No, it was a sandwich
      A giant hero sandwich!
I was starving: it was lunchtime.
    I had no snack.
And da Vinci's "Last Supper" flashed
      before me.
What were they eating?
    Were there any grapes?
I felt ashamed
    that the spirit had not moved me—
removed the hollow pit in my stomach
    until Brother Camillus asked me later
what I had seen in my meditation.
    "A sandwich," I confessed

with the honesty of a Catholic schoolgirl
      though I knew he had a sense
           of humor.
He laughed. "You know what Gandhi
      said about the hungry poor—
The first spiritual vision of God
      they will have
           is a loaf of bread!"
He moved on, but I knew then
      my spiritual life
           was right on target.

PAST LIVES

I saw a woman wrapped in a black shawl
walking over a great limestone plain.
Then I was at New Grange in ancient
times. I was dressed in rags,
and a tall ragged man with a crozier staff
greeted me. I entered the tomb alone.
Felt my way down the narrow passage,
touching the incised spirals on the walls
until I found myself in a large domed room.
There I took off my rags,
lay down on the earthen floor,
and spent the night. The next morning
a sliver of light entered the passage.
I arose, dressed myself in a bright
yellow garment and butterfly cape
and emerged from the tomb like a queen.

A horse awaited me. I rode like
the wind, but the stallion soon stumbled
and fell, and I had to walk clear across Ireland
to Galway. I was in tatters again.
I found myself in an ale house in Galway.
An old crone came in. She took me
up a spiral staircase to a high stone tower.
I wondered whether I'd have to throw
down my hair like Rapunzel to get out.
I spun myself a new set of clothes,
a red dress and a purple cape,
then realized I wasn't locked in. I descended
the staircase and walked out the door.

A boat awaited me in the bay,
and I sailed to the Aran Islands.
I saw the woman wrapped in a black shawl

walking across the great limestone slab
as I walked to Dun Aengus, a fort
on the edge of a cliff. I peered over
the edge at the water which beckoned below
and I fell. A giant bird like Emily Carr's
great raven swooped under my back and I soared
in the air. The meditation gong
rang, and I was back in Assumption Hall,
shaking my head in disbelief.

"I don't believe in romantic fairy tales," I said.
My waking hours had just been spent
with policemen and firemen, hell bent
on writing from their lives to earn college credit
in "Stress Management," "Death and Dying,"
and the "Sociology of Rape."
"You need the escape," said Penny.
"You dream in archetypes."
I saw transformation after transformation.
My policemen and firemen
were becoming students once again,
and I, an academic counselor,
a character in *The Mists of Avalon*.

THE CORKS

She told me
Bridget told me
That's what they say
in Ireland
"She's got the corks."
That means
when your lips
get all pursed up
but you're fit
to burst wide open inside
and you're all bottled up
and kapowie and kapowie
and you can hardly
keep it in
and your lips get purser and purser
and kapowie and kapowie inside
and and
"You've got the corks."

CONFESSIONS OF A COUNSELOR

All I know is:
I did not marry a Rumanian gypsy when I was 19 years old
I do not have six kids
I did not wake up in a body bag in Vietnam
My husband was not killed in a light plane crash
          when I was 33 years old
My mother does not have lupus
I do not have breast cancer, bulimia, anorexia,
          or manic depressive disorder
My wife does not have a borderline personality
My husband does not beat me
I have not lived behind a dumpster in my car
nor am I responsible for a 2.5 million dollar budget
          or a LAN network
My ex-husband did not die of AIDS
I am not a policeman with a baby face who infiltrated
          Operation Rescue
I did not expose a Munchausen's syndrome baby killer
I am not an addict, cocaine sniffer, alcohol abuser
I did not die under the wheels of a Muni bus
          and return to life
I did not leave Cuba in exile as a child
I did not go to Thailand as a magician
          and live with a transsexual
I did not lose ten friends from AIDS
I did not flunk my English Composition test three times
          so I could not graduate
I did not lose my job at Mervyn's, Pac Bell, Apple, or TWA
I did not escape Poland and have to leave my baby behind
My husband did not start a cult and torture small animals
My answering machine does not say I am out
          creating sunshine
but, by God, I wish it did.

HOPE

Juan wants to know
whether I can read his 2,000 word paper.
Search for spelling errors
before he turns it in to his new teacher.

Mrs. Morgan wants to know
whether I can talk to her young daughter,
fresh out of high school
about a career as a poet.

Robert wants to know
why we are only reading about
men who turn into beetles, women
who are stoned to death, and catatonic clerks.

"Is there any hope?" he says.
To the man who misspells
I say "No."
"That's o.k.," he says,
"I'm getting a computer, anyway."

I talk to Mrs. Morgan's daughter
in a coffee shop.
She tells me her mother is a clerk
for the Oakland Police.

Then asks me if I ever perceive a shadow
a certain way on the wall
when drinking my hot chocolate.
I have to tell her "No."

To the man who wants hope, I laugh.
I am a poet

who lives in a basement.
I've been a catatonic clerk.

Melville gives me a thrill.
Kafka was one of my lovers.
I am only a substitute
and do not have the right answers.

RE-ENTRY COUNSELOR

My students slip back into themselves
as kids, "the bad boy" in school,
the Asian-American now married computer whiz
who disappointed his mother
by not becoming an engineer like his three older
        brothers,
or a "chemist of sorts" like his younger sister.

We've got all sorts in our classes,
the chiropractor whom the nurses gave a baby shower
and when he didn't invite his wife to class,
they rang her up and said, "Where are you?"
and she came on down and the nurses said,
"Don't let him give you any shit!"

This was all reported by their instructor,
who said she was definitely not the instigator
of all this. My job is GOSSIP.
I'm like the hairdresser of the college.
People clip their split ends and dump them
in my lap. I sift through their hairy tales
and wonder what the truth is.

I sit on the ends of telephone lines and wonder
which lines are connected, which are
burdened down by fat, black desert crows,
which are ringing with people's souls.
Sometimes only the great telephone
operator in the sky knows: Ernestine the Great
with her nasal pitch and voice piece.

By the Great Goddess, the lines are all busy
in my mind. I'm disconnected now
while babies are born and die

in the same day—this is a metaphor.
One office visit with me and the doers become
        introverts,
the introverts become great writers,
and the great writers get 30 college units in the blink
of an eye. Who says counseling is not effective?

And if they tell me they were abused kids
and their dad took barbed wire
and raked it across their legs,
I believe it by the lines in their faces,
each one carved when they were a child,
once invisible, now great gaping gullies
that only tears could fill and no plastic surgeon

could repair. They need flesh not plastic
to cure their wounds, and if they became mystics
and purged their souls, they would need no more
        suffering
to make them ready to receive the godhead.
They've done it all when they were young, and I
        wonder
sometimes, when they sit in front of me and talk
so dignifiedly of their past,

I wonder how they survived
and what small child sits alone
in a highchair at night, the moon looking down,
and howls her brains out,
and I wonder why her own children never hear her.

THE SEMINAR

It was one of those all day seminars
where you pay a small fortune
to have someone give you a shot in the arm
for job burnout.
This one was for women:
Confidence, Credibility, & Composure.
I imagined someone inspecting our hems,
spots on skirts, and having us
walk across a stage
with a book on our head.
Instead, we got Carolyn,
a feisty, short woman
in a royal blue power suit
with a street accent from Joisey.
"Ladies," she said, "I think it's
appropriate to share this with you.
From age 18 to 38, I was a nun.
Could anybody tell?"
We all stared at her dumbfounded.
She was hustling power books for women's success.
Was now a corporate trainer with shoulder pads
and buzz words buzzing off her tongue.
And I think all of us to a woman
imagined a wilting flower
in a convent
suddenly transformed into a sassy
corporate dynamo with blue eye shadow.
"Ladies, I was very depressed,
even suicidal, was in therapy for two years.
When I finally made the decision to leave
the convent, I was at peace."
And there she was, superwoman
underneath the habit
and we all felt, to a woman,

if she can do it, well so can we.
And all of us, to a woman
undid our tortured selves,
stripped off our deadly habits
of procrastination and tiny voices
and inaction and declared ourselves
the new leaders of America.
And all we could remember
when we went back to St. Mary's
was not confidence, credibility, and composure,
but an ex-nun
with a Joisey accent saying,
"Ladies, did you ever see
a woman enter a room,
impeccably groomed, beautifully dressed and poised,
and see a small knot of women
in a corner saying
'Who does that bitch think she is?'
But you know what BITCH stands for, ladies?
Being In Total Control of Herself!"
We all howled
and we all thought
if that bitch
of an ex-nun can do it,
by God, WE CAN TOO!

BOOK CLUB

Mary Arcana says to me,
"You look familiar."
I look into her clear blue eyes,
then, at her dark hair.
She looks familiar, too,
but we've never met.

We hit it off
and later when I suggest
How the Irish Saved Civilization
to read in our book club,
she says, "Are you Irish?
I knew you were.
You look like you went
to Catholic school."

"Why?" I say.
"You have those rosy cheeks.
You'd look good in a habit!"
"So would you," I say,
and we explode in laughter.
She's only a quarter,
and so am I, but
we both have that
Catholic schoolgirl look
even though I'm 52
and she's years younger.

Helene wants to get in on the action.
She's Irish too—
more like 100%
filled with O'Briens
and Pendergasts and Maxwells.
She says her mother was placed

on the church altar
when she was a babe
and dedicated to the Virgin Mary.

She had to wear blue
her first seven years
and to this day, guess what her
mother's favorite color is—
Blue—Yes! And Helene's—
Blue, Yes!
No, this was not in Ireland
but in Philadelphia, U.S.A.

Now we're all in Oakland/Berkeley,
assimilated, or are we?
What is this secret club
of crazy, educated Irish women
you can spot across a room
by complexion and bearing
and rosy cheeks
so you all seem like sisters,
the ones in habits
        and without?

THE DRESS

Today at St. Mary's College
I wore a dress
for the first time
in 8 years.
I hid in my office
I was so self-conscious.
Didn't want anyone to see me
and then of course,
I finally had to come out,
and boy, did I get the remarks.
Sarah said I'd "sold out,"
and Cynthia said, I was dressed up
from my ankles up.
If I had on Birkenstocks
(which I didn't)
I'd still be my old self,
and Pat said I should dress
like that more often,
and Bev said I looked really nice today—
Oops, I mean you always look nice,
but the dress is flattering,
and really it was, but I kept
emphasizing it was culottes really,
and Sarah came up to see whether
she was too harsh,
saying I'd "sold out,"
and I told everyone
it was $19.99
Ross Dress for Less
Hot tip given by Janis.
They got in good stuff recently,
and probably even
cartoon Cathy could find
a good dress at Ross

Dress for Less,
but when I got home
even though I looked really pretty,
I tore out of that dress
(dry clean only
hot drive home)
and pulled on khaki pants
and a yellow cotton t-shirt
all washable
and no I don't have Birkenstocks anymore,
but today I wish I did
so I could just be
a Berkeley poet again
and not feel like
an 8 year old tomboy
in her first real dress
grown up
pluck your eyebrows next,
but eat your hearts out
office mates.
I'm thin
and I look good
in a dress,
look good in a dress.
Woo woo—take a good look!
Could be the last time
you'll see me
in a dress.
Could be the last time.
On the other hand,
Woo, woo!
I might just get another one.

ENGLISH TEST

I have to tell her, no,
her essay will not do
for college senior level writing.
I gently probe and find,
yes, her first language was Tagalog
for twenty years.
She shrinks at first,
gets smaller in her chair
but then I see the fight
rising from within
and the protest begins.
No, she did not realize
she would have to hand that paper in.
She just did it that morning.
She is taking a grammar course
on the side.
She will get a tutor.
She will do anything to stay in.
She has to.
She is supporting three others
in the Philippines
and her 73 year old mother here.
She and her mother work weekends
and nights as janitors.
My ancestors rise before me
with their Irish accents
as they clean houses,
work in mills, mines,
plant vines, anything to bring
a sister, a brother closer
to their new home.
"Can you support yourselves
as janitors on weekends?" I ask.
"I also make $40,000 a year

at my regular job," she adds.
I nearly gasp.
Her ambition is as palpable
as a vacuum cleaner in her hand
which sweeps me in.
She is the tide of new America,
and I am on her side.

PATRICK KAVANAGH
MARRIES

PATRICK KAVANAGH MARRIES KERRY AT BEESON HILL MUSHROOM FARM

For Patrick Kavanagh
and Kerry LeFever

Patrick promises never
to treat Kerry like a mushroom,
and one of his friends toasts him,
"May all your ups and downs
be only in bed!"
and Kerry sings to him
the most beautiful song
and as she sings
he looks deep into her eyes
with such wonder
with the same eyes he had
as a baby
so of course I cried
because I could feel the love
or was it his surprise
that his wife sang to him
on their wedding
day underneath a bower
in front of poppies
and blue corn flowers
fertilized by their hens
on the former site
of their chicken coop.

And when the ceremony was over,
and we all clapped and signed their scroll,
they took a walk
around the pine tree-lined path
at the back of their property

for another rite of passage.
They emerged looking
only slightly mussed
with Kerry in her purple satin dress
and Patrick in his blue green vest
—O love—
and someone said
they were going to call
their first child Shasta
—O love—
—O love—
Shasta Kavanagh
though they live beneath Mount Hood
in the shadow
of the volcano.

Their cakes were three huge mushroom-
shaped pods
sitting on three large stems.
They were chocolate
raspberry and white
and there was a whole
roasted pig on a table nearby
with a severed head.
I could see its teeth
holding the apple
and its green plastic eyes.
The butcher said someone
might be offended by real ones
at this Irish wedding
with the best shiitake mushroom and zucchini
lasagna I have ever eaten
for the vegetarians
and the greasy, well-cooked pig
for the meat eaters
and potatoes and salad for all.

This wedding feast
mirrors no Irish famine,
This wedding feast
of eat hardy

Irish music
tin whistle, guitar
and Bride and Bridegroom
in the center of a circle
while Kerry's women's choir
and we guests gather round
to sing them a peace song,
Peace to the marriage.
Then Patrick and Kerry
lead us in a spiral dance.
We hold hands snaking
inward in a spiral
till Patrick suddenly turns
and spirals out
and we all pass by each
other in the opposite
direction in a new
marriage of eyes and I
wonder whether neolithic farmers
5,000 years ago in Ireland
joined hands in the same way
re-enacting the spirals
of the Goddess.

Patrick has a mushroom farm
the only one of the Kavanaghs
to get "his farm"
though an odd one
with huge red autoclave
to sterilize his sawdust
out of which, when sown

with spores,
will sprout
delicate shiitake mushrooms
which may one day find their way
beside your steak
or in your veggie pasta.
"I will never
treat you like a mushroom"
says Pat to his bride.
Kerry will keep her own name.
He will never treat her
like a mushroom—
though he tends them well
they are soon sold
to a broker—
so thank God for that!
My nephew has
a sly sense of humor
along with large, soulful eyes.

I've heard a lot about
Irish wakes, little about Irish weddings
so let this occasion
stand
for the New Age Irish wedding
in America
where the theme color is purple
and the trees and grass are green
and fertility
is in the air
and I hope a new little mushroom
Shasta Kavanagh
is about to bloom.

August 19, 1995
Beavercreek, Oregon

About the Author

Judy Wells was born in San Francisco, California, the great-granddaughter of Irish immigrant Edward Rodgers (MacCrory), from Gortin, Co. Tyrone, and Letitia Kinney of Philadelphia. She received her B.A. from Stanford University and her Ph.D. in Comparative Literature from the University of California, Berkeley, and is currently an Academic Counselor in the School of Extended Education at St. Mary's College, Moraga, California. In addition to her sixth poetry collection, *Everything Irish*, she has written a series of essays entitled *A Vegetarian in Ireland*, based on three trips to Ireland in search of her roots. She is also the author of *The Calling*, poems on 20th century women artists, and *The Part-Time Teacher*, a comic tale of her odyssey as a part-time college instructor in the San Francisco Bay Area. She lives in Berkeley.